THE EASY
WAY TO
STUDY
COLORS

New
Edition

By
Ezeagu E.
Stephen

The author
Series of
book

1. The Lizard
   and Rat

2. International
Standard Road
      Signs

 3. The Critical
Life Skills, etc.

ISBN:
978-978-
953-162-2

Colour
samples

Front
contents
cover

Purple
=Secondary
colour
Blue purple =
Tertiary
Blue = Primary
Blue Green =
Tertiary
Secondary =
Green

Yellow Green
= Tertiary
Yellow =
Primary
Orange Yellow
= Tertiary

Orange =
Secondary

Orange Red =
Tertiary

Red Purple =
Tertiary

Back
contents

Color mixing styles

About the
book

The easy way to study colours is specifically designed for everyone who have interest of color and need to know more of its creative designs.

It will also help
students of all
class to improve
t h e i r   c o l o r
knowledge and
a p p l i c a t i o n
w   h   e   n
necessary.

It's also throw
more lights on
how you can
differentiate
between color
of paint and
color of light.

You will also get to know about how it is being illustrated as for light aspect.

Additive
color mixing

Additive color mixing is for light. In the book, the p r a c t i c a l illustration is done in a way y o u c a n comprehend it.

Additive color
mixing is also the
reflection of light.

Subtractive
color mixing

Subtractive
color mixing
is color for
paint.

In subtractive
color mixing, you
will get to know
how to mix two or
more different
color paints to
get a wonderful
paint mixture.